ALPHA
GUIDE

YOUNGER YOUTH

ISBN: 978 1 905887 95 8

Scripture quotations (marked NIV) taken from the Holy Bible, New International Version Anglicised. Copyright © 1979, 1984, 2011 Biblica, formerly International Bible Society. Used by permission of Hodder & Stoughton Publishers, an Hachette UK company. All rights reserved. 'NIV' is a registered trademark of Biblica. UK trademark number 1448790. Scripture quotations marked (ERV) are taken from the HOLY BIBLE: EASY-TO-READ VERSION © 2006 by World Bible Translation Center, Inc. and used by permission. Scripture quotations marked (NIrV) are taken from the Holy Bible, New International Reader's Version®, NIrV® Copyright © 1995, 1996, 1998 by Biblica, Inc.™ Used by permission of Zondervan. All rights reserved worldwide. www.zondervan.com The "NIrV" and "New International Reader's Version" are trademarks registered in the United States Patent and Trademark Office by Biblica, Inc.™ Scripture taken from The Message. Copyright © 1993, 1994, 1995, 1996, 2000, 2001, 2002. Used by permission of NavPress Publishing Group. Scripture quotations marked (NLT) are taken from the Holy Bible, New Living Translation, copyright © 1996, 2004, 2007 by Tyndale House Foundation. Used by permission of Tyndale House Publishers, Inc., Carol Stream, Illinois 60188. All rights reserved.

Designed by Samuel Nudds for Alpha International

Published by Alpha International, HTB Brompton Road, London, SW7 1JA

Email: publications@alpha.org
alpha.org
@alphacourse

CONTENTS

WELCOME

There are so many questions in life – some of them will be in your head already (like, why can't I lick my elbow?) and some of them you simply won't have thought of yet (is it ever going to be possible to build a giant elevator to the moon one day?). (OK you may have thought of that one already – but you know what we mean.)

Some of them are pretty easy to answer (can I do long division in my head?), or at least easy to find out the answer to (what is consistently the biggest-selling book in the world?), whereas some of them are really, really tricky and we might never get a perfect answer (what happens when I pray?).

It's good to ask questions. It doesn't mean we have to be able to answer them all.

Lots of the questions that people find really tricky to answer are actually to do with God. So we decided to look at some of them on Alpha – Youth and we've put this guide together so you have something to look at and write your thoughts in.

It's all part of the journey to help **YOU** find out what **YOU** really think.

CHRISTIANITY: BORING, UNTRUE, IRRELEVANT?

HAVE YOU EVER WONDERED WHAT LIFE IS ALL ABOUT?

Christianity is named after **Jesus Christ** who lived about 2000 years ago. Jesus said that God exists and has a purpose for our lives.

Ever thought about that?

Is Christianity boring?

* Jesus says he came to give us life, but not a boring life at all – in fact a life that's really full! Jesus said, 'I am ... **the life**.' (John 14:6)

Is Christianity untrue?

- Truth isn't such a popular idea today. Jesus said, 'I am ... **the truth**' (John 14:6). He didn't say a truth, but **the** truth

Is Christianity irrelevant?

- Jesus said, 'I am **the way**' (John 14:6). With Jesus, we can expect a life full of purpose, fun, direction and meaning

  It doesn't mean easy, but it does mean

FULL.

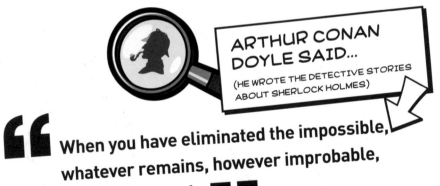

BART SIMPSON SAID...

"What if you're a really good person, but you get into a really, really bad fight and your leg gets gangrene and it has to be amputated. Will it be waiting for you in heaven?"

ARTHUR CONAN DOYLE SAID...
(HE WROTE THE DETECTIVE STORIES ABOUT SHERLOCK HOLMES)

"When you have eliminated the impossible, whatever remains, however improbable, must be the truth."

Jesus Christ said:

" I am the

WAY and the

TRUTH

and the

LIFE. "

WHAT THE BIBLE SAYS

[John 14:6]

IF IT TURNED OUT THAT GOD EXISTS AND YOU COULD ASK GOD ONE QUESTION...

...WHAT WOULD IT BE?

Why don't you write down your question for God here, and see if it gets answered during the course?

A SPACE TO THINK

OR MAYBE YOU'VE GOT LOTS OF QUESTIONS? IF YOU WRITE THEM DOWN, YOU COULD KEEP THE BOOK TILL YOU'RE 70 AND SEE HOW MANY GET ANSWERED.

OR, YOU COULD GO AND ASK SOMEONE WHO'S SEVENTY AND SEE WHAT THEIR QUESTION IS.

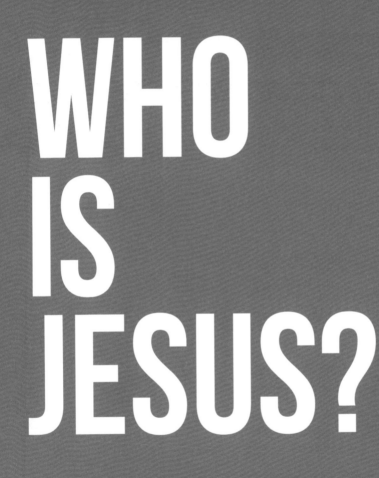

WHO IS JESUS?

SESSION

17

WHAT IS IT ABOUT THIS PERSON, JESUS? PEOPLE ARE STILL TALKING ABOUT HIM MORE THAN 2,000 YEARS AFTER HE LIVED.

Did Jesus actually exist?

Most scholars, whether Christians or not, agree on the following points about Jesus Christ:

- He was a **Jewish** man, born in Bethlehem in Judea around 4 BC

- He was famous for being a great teacher and miracle worker

- He was crucified (killed by being hung on a cross) by the **Romans**

- His followers believed he was the Son of God and that he came back to life after his death and burial

Was Jesus more than just a 'good man?'

Jesus made some pretty big claims about himself and did incredible stuff:

- He said that anyone who had seen him had **seen God** (John 14:9)

- He said 'I am the resurrection and the life' – meaning he would beat death for us and give us life that lasts forever [John 11:25]

- He went around forgiving sins and healing people – in Mark 2:5 he said to someone, 'Your sins are forgiven.' People believed that only God could forgive sin

So was Jesus mad, bad or God?

We have *three* possibilities to think about:

1. Jesus wasn't God, and knew he wasn't: **so he was lying. He was a fraudster, a bad person**

2. Jesus wasn't God but just thought he was: **so he was a deluded, mad person**

3. Jesus was telling the truth: **he really is God**

What do you think?

- Jesus coming back to life three days after he died (called the resurrection) supports his claims. If it's true, it is proof that **he really is God**

LOOK! ⊗

There are over 300 Old Testament prophecies (predictions) about things like Jesus' birth, his mother, his death and his burial – and every single one of them came true.

19

CONSPIRACY THEORIES ABOUT JESUS' DEATH ON THE CROSS

Coming back to life three days after you've died is pretty incredible and definitely not normal – so it's understandable that people have a lot to say on the matter! There are many different theories about what actually happened.

These facts about Jesus are agreed by everybody, believer and sceptic alike:

FACT 1   The Romans crucified Jesus

FACT 2   Jesus' body was placed in a tomb that was closed with a large stone and guarded by soldiers

FACT 3   On the third day after Jesus' death, the tomb was found to be empty

FACT 4   The belief that Jesus had been raised from the dead spread through the known world

Conspiracy theory one – Jesus didn't really die

Some people have argued that Jesus didn't really die on the cross – he only passed out from the pain and exhaustion.

They believe that when he was taken off the cross and laid down in a comfortable position in a cool tomb he simply recovered consciousness, got up and walked off.

Conspiracy theory two – the disciples stole the body

Some people believe that in the middle of the night the disciples crept up and overpowered the sleepy Roman guards.

They then rolled the stone away from the entrance to the tomb, picked up Jesus' lifeless body and disappeared into the night.

They started the rumours that Jesus had risen from the dead in order to make themselves seem more important. Throughout the rest of their lives they never let on to anyone what they had done.

Conspiracy theory three – the authorities secretly removed Jesus' body

Some people think that the Jewish and Roman authorities worked together to steal and get rid of Jesus' body; perhaps because they didn't want the tomb to become a religious shrine or holy place constantly crowded with Jesus' old followers.

CONSPIRACY THEORIES

They simply took the body and buried it somewhere else, somewhere secret.

PROBLEMS WITH THESE CONSPIRACY THEORIES

Conspiracy theory one – Jesus didn't really die

Even before being hung on the cross Jesus was brutally beaten and tortured.

Roman soldiers, who knew from experience when their victims were dead, carried out the crucifixion.

Dead bodies in those days were wrapped like mummies in cloth.

To escape the tomb Jesus would have had to get out of the grave clothes, roll away a heavy stone and fight the soldiers.

EVIDENCE EVIDENCE EVIDENCE EVIDENCE EV

Conspiracy theory two – the disciples stole the body

The disciples were scared and confused; it's unlikely they were thinking of a daring rescue operation.

It is very unlikely that the disciples could have physically overpowered the Roman soldiers guarding the tomb.

It is believed that all the disciples were eventually killed for their belief in Jesus' resurrection. Surely at least one of them would have confessed the truth to save his own skin?

Conspiracy theory three – the authorities secretly removed Jesus' body

The authorities hated the fast spreading belief that Jesus was alive and had risen from the dead.

If they'd had the body, or had known where it was, they would simply have produced it and thrown it down in a public place to prove to everyone that Jesus really was dead.

They didn't do this, so we have to assume that they didn't have the body.

One more thing...

None of these theories can account for the fact that over 500 people are reported to have seen Jesus alive in the weeks following his crucifixion.

C.S. LEWIS SAID...
(C.S. LEWIS WROTE THE NARNIA BOOKS)

"

A man who was merely a man and said the sort of things Jesus said wouldn't be a great moral teacher; he'd either be insane or else he'd be the devil of hell. You must make your choice. Either this man was and is the Son of God or else insane or something worse. But don't let us come up with any patronising nonsense about his being a great human teacher. He hasn't left that open to us. He didn't intend to.

"

Jesus Christ said:

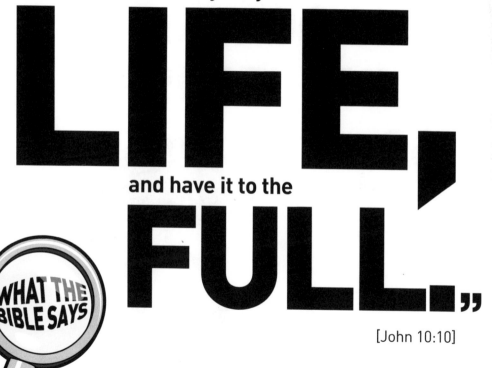

" I have come that they may have **LIFE,** and have it to the **FULL.** "

WHAT THE BIBLE SAYS

[John 10:10]

WHO DO YOU THINK JESUS IS?

- What do you think it would be like if Jesus was your teacher?

- Do you think it would be interesting?

- Do you think what he said over 2000 years ago would be the same as he would say to us today?

A SPACE TO THINK

I THINK JESUS WAS ...

WHY DID JESUS DIE?

SESSION 2

WHY WOULD ANYONE WEAR A CROSS – AN INSTRUMENT OF DEATH AND TORTURE – AS JEWELLERY?

What's the problem?

- The problem is sin. In other words, we've all 'messed up'

- The Bible tells us that God really wants to have a **perfect friendship** with us

- God created us perfect – without any bad stuff. As long as we are clean, we can have a relationship with him

- But the problem is that none of us is perfect. We've all messed up. And this **sin separates** us from God

LOOK!

Jesus said: 'If the Son sets you free, you are truly free.'
(John 8:36, NLT)

What's the solution?

- God's Son **Jesus** was the only human who never did anything wrong – he **was perfect**

- When Jesus died on the cross, he was given the punishment that we actually deserve for the stuff we do wrong. It's a tricky thing to understand, but he died for us

- So that means we can now **be free** to have that relationship, or friendship, with God. We're not separated, by our mess, from God anymore

What's the result?

- **Jesus overcame death** – he died on the cross, but then came back to life. You can read about it in Mark 16 in the Bible

- **If we believe** that Jesus died on the cross for us, and if we say sorry for the things that we have done wrong, we can start to have an exciting relationship with God

MAX, 11 AND JONNY, 13...

" What Jesus did on the cross is a bit like this: Everyone starts off wearing a clean t-shirt, and when you do something bad, it's as if your t-shirt gets dirty. Jesus always has a clean t-shirt because he never did anything bad. When he died on the cross for us he took off his clean t-shirt, gave it to us to put on and put on our dirty ones. Jesus wipes our slate clean and gives us a fresh start. "

God

LOVED THE WORLD

WHAT THE BIBLE SAYS

so much that he gave his one and only Son. Anyone who believes in him will not die but will have eternal life.

[John 3:16, NIrV]

JOHN 3:16

LOOK! ⊗

Sometimes in big crowds you'll see people walking around with John 3:16 on a placard.

33

HOW DO YOU FEEL ABOUT THE IDEA THAT GOD WANTS TO BE IN RELATIONSHIP WITH YOU?

A SPACE TO THINK

WHY DON'T YOU SPEND A FEW MINUTES THINKING ABOUT THAT AND WRITE DOWN YOUR THOUGHTS ...

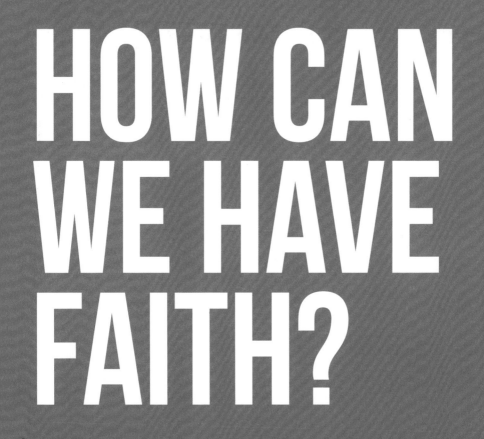

HOW CAN WE HAVE FAITH?

SESSION

3

DOES GOING TO CHURCH MAKE YOU A CHRISTIAN?

Christian faith is based on three people: God the Father, Jesus (God's Son) and the Holy Spirit. This is called the 'Trinity'.

Each person of the Trinity is important in making our faith secure (a bit like three legs on a stool means it won't fall over).

What the Father promises

- The Bible is a written **record of God's love for us**. Even if we aren't feeling loved, the good news is, we can know that God loves us because it says so in the Bible.

- God promises that he will come in to our lives and help us – **all we have to do is ask him**!

- God promises that he will be with us forever (Matthew 28:20). He promises to give us **eternal life** with him in heaven (John 10:28)

LOOK! ⊗

Water, ice and steam are each different, but they are all H_2O. It's a bit like that with the Trinity: the Father, Son and Holy Spirit are three people, yet they are all God.

What Jesus did

- **Jesus was unique**. By dying on the cross, he made it possible for us to have a relationship with God. **He took the blame** for everything we've ever done wrong

- Because of what Jesus did, every time we do something wrong, we can sincerely pray to God to **forgive us** and he says that he will

What the Spirit does

- The Holy Spirit is the presence of God in the world and in our lives

- When someone becomes a Christian, the Holy Spirit comes to live in them and help them. This means we begin to live and act more like Jesus did, which is brilliant!

- The ways we start to change, like our behavior and our thoughts, are described in the Bible as the 'fruit' of the Holy Spirit (Galatians 5:22). But it takes time – **just like real fruit growing**

Conclusion

- Becoming a Christian involves faith, but not blind faith

- Faith is daring to believe God's promises

> **LOOK!** ✖
>
> Jesus doesn't force anyone to let him in to their life – the choice is ours.

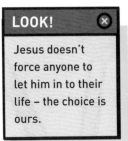

Our feelings go up and down depending on the day, the week and the mood we're in. But we don't base our faith on how we are feeling day-by-day, although that is important. We can base our faith on what God promises us in the Bible.

Do you not know?
Have you not heard?

The Lord is the

EVERLASTING
GOD

the Creator of the ends of the earth. He will not grow tired or weary, and his understanding no one can fathom.

[Isaiah 40:28]

WHAT THE BIBLE SAYS

IS THERE MORE TO MAKING A DECISION THAN JUST WHAT YOU 'FEEL'?

Lean Upon

A STORY TO THINK ABOUT

John Patton was a Scot who travelled all the way from Scotland to a group of islands in the South West Pacific so that he could tell the tribal people about Jesus. He wanted to translate the Bible into their tribal language.

The islanders were cannibals (people who eat other people!) and his life was in constant danger. When Patton tried to translate the Bible into the tribal language he found there was no word for 'belief' or 'trust'. Nobody trusted anybody else (not surprising really!) and as a result they didn't have the word in their language.

Finally, when one of the tribal people came in to his study, he thought of a way to find the word he was looking for. Patton raised both his feet off of the ground, leant back in his chair and asked the man, 'What am I doing now?' The servant gave him a word that means 'to lean your whole weight upon'. This was the word Patton used in his translation of the Bible.

That's what faith is – leaning all our weight on God – putting all our trust in him and letting him support us. It's saying, 'Ok Jesus, I really want to hear what you think about stuff. What do you think I should do? Will you guide me? I choose to listen.'

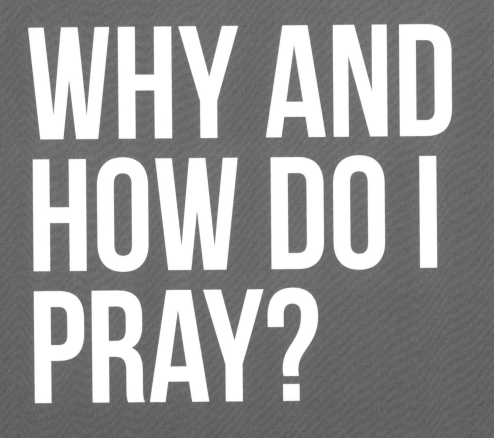

WHY AND HOW DO I PRAY?

SESSION

4

OFTEN, WHEN BAD THINGS HAPPEN, PEOPLE DECIDE TO PRAY. WHY?

What is Prayer?

- Prayer is like having a **'speed dial'** to God

- We pray:

  - **to the Father** – God is our 'dad' and he is also holy and powerful (Matthew 6:6)

  - **through the Son** – Jesus is our link to God the Father (Ephesians 2:18)

  - **by the Holy Spirit** – the Holy Spirit helps us to pray (Romans 8:26)

Why Pray?

- **Jesus prayed** to God – and he told us to pray as well (Luke 6:12)

- Talking to God is how we develop a relationship with him – imagine having a friend that you never actually talk to! That would never work!

- Prayer really does **change** situations (Matthew 7:7–11)

Does God always answer my prayers?

- God's answer might be 'yes', 'no', or he might say, 'wait'. But **he always hears us**; he would never just ignore us

- God can't answer all prayers with a 'yes' – if you think about it, both teams can't win the same **football match**. And sometimes God just knows what's best for us (even if we don't agree at the time)

- We might need to ask ourselves if there is stuff we need to deal with first. Maybe we need to **forgive someone**, or we need to ask for forgiveness. Perhaps our motives are wrong (we are asking for something selfishly). These things can make it hard for us to hear what God is saying

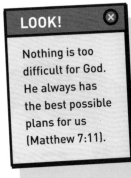

LOOK! ⊗

Nothing is too difficult for God. He always has the best possible plans for us (Matthew 7:11).

How to pray?

- We can pray anytime, anywhere. Try **THIS SIMPLE PRAYER (TSP)**:

    T – Thank you: start by thinking of at least one thing to thank God for

    S – Sorry: say sorry for what you have done wrong

    P – Please: ask God for what you, and other people, need. Ask for help

Jesus said
This, then, is how you should pray:

OUR FATHER in heaven,

HALLOWED BE your name,

your **KINGDOM COME**,

your will be done **ON EARTH** as it is in heaven.

GIVE US today our daily bread,

FORGIVE US our debts,

AS WE also **HAVE FORGIVEN** our debtors.

And **LEAD US** not into temptation,

but **DELIVER US** from the evil one.

[Matthew 6:9–13]

WHAT DO YOU THINK IS THE BEST THING ABOUT THE IDEA OF PRAYER?

Some people find it easier to write their prayers down – like a letter to God.

You could try writing a prayer now using the T S P guide to help you.

A SPACE TO THINK

DEAR GOD,

Thank you for _____

_____

Sorry about _____

_____

Please help me with _____

_____

PLEASE HELP MY FRIEND/FAMILY MEMBER _____ WITH _____

_____

IN JESUS' NAME,

AMEN

WHY AND HOW SHOULD I READ THE BIBLE?

SESSION

5

CAN A BOOK FROM 2,000 YEARS AGO STILL HAVE ANY RELEVANCE TO OUR LIVES TODAY?

HOLY BIBLE

An instruction manual for life

- The Bible is a **big** book, but it's exciting – it's the story of God, his love for the world and the humans who live in it. In fact, there is sex, romance, war, revenge, love, sacrifice and murder!

- God has designed the Bible to be **like a compass** for us – it provides us with direction in life

- It's not an ordinary book. We talk about it being **'God-breathed'**, meaning, even though humans wrote the words, it was God who inspired them to know what to write (2 Timothy 3:15–17)

A way to relationship

- The Bible is the main way that **God speaks** to us and guides us

How do we hear God speak through the Bible?

- Choose a place where you are relaxed and where you won't be disturbed or get distracted

- **Begin by praying** – ask God to speak to you through what you read. Why not start by reading the story of Jesus – in the books of Matthew, Mark, Luke or John

- Ask yourself three key questions about the text: What does this say? What does this mean? What does this mean for my life?

SIR ISAAC NEWTON SAID...
(HE WAS A SCIENTIST, FAMOUS FOR HIS WORK ON GRAVITY)

" I have a fundamental belief in the Bible as the Word of God, written by men who were inspired. I study the Bible daily. "

PSALM 119:105 SAYS...
(THE MESSAGE)

" By your words I can see where I'm going; they throw a beam of light on my dark path. "

ALL
SCRIPTURE IS
GOD-BREATHED.

[2 Timothy 3:16]

WHAT THE BIBLE SAYS

57

IF THE BIBLE IS A BIT LIKE AN INSTRUCTION MANUAL FOR LIFE... DO YOU THINK THAT RESTRICTS OR INCREASES FREEDOM?

Smuggled Bibles

Nicky Gumbel, the person who pioneered Alpha, told this story:

When I was twenty-one we went on a family trip to the Soviet Union. I had read that Christians were persecuted there and it was very hard to get hold of Bibles.

Full of enthusiasm, I wrote to an organisation that I knew helped smuggle Bibles into places like that. I sent them some money and said that I wanted to take some Bibles with me when I went to Russia.

I got two replies. The official reply read 'So sorry, we can't supply you with any Bibles it's illegal to take them into Russia, and we suggest that you don't do so.' The second was the unofficial reply: I saw on my doorstep an unmarked brown paper parcel containing Russian Bibles. So, feeling like James Bond, I packed these Bibles into my case.

When I got to Russia, we went into a church. In those days, the KGB (the Russian Secret Police) often went into the church to spy. I tried to spot someone who looked like a genuine Christian. I saw a man, probably in his sixties, whose face was really shining. So I followed him out of the church and down the street where it was completely deserted.

There, I took out of my pocket a complete Russian Bible and handed it to him. In turn, he took out of his pocket a copy of just the New Testament, probably a hundred years old as the pages were threadbare. When he saw a whole Bible, he started literally jumping and dancing for joy. He hugged me! I didn't speak any Russian and he didn't speak any English but we ran up and down the streets, jumping for joy! That man knew that he had in his hands something truly unique.

HOW DOES GOD GUIDE US?

SESSION

6

WHAT DO YOU THINK YOU'LL BE DOING WHEN YOU ARE 25? WHAT DECISIONS WILL YOU HAVE TO MAKE ALONG THE WAY?

Christians try to follow the ways God guides them.

If we are struggling with a particular problem and don't know what to do, God promises to show us – we just need to ask and then listen to him.

So how does God guide us?

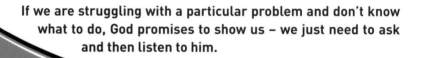

Through the Bible

- If we read the Bible regularly, then God will often remind us of a particular bit we have read at just the right time to guide us in a **decision**

By the Holy Spirit

- The Holy Spirit helps us to **hear** God's voice. God speaks to us as we pray – perhaps through an overall feeling, or a sense of what is right. We can check this with someone we trust if we're not sure

Through advice from others

- There are times when we need help to make the right choices in life. God has given us **friends and family** to help us make important decisions

Through common sense

- God has given us a **conscience and a brain**, and he wants us to use them! If something seems like a stupid or hurtful idea, then it probably is!

Through random signs

- God sometimes uses **'coincidences'** and random stuff to speak to us as well. So if you think a significant 'coincidence' has happened, **ask God** if he was showing you anything and check with someone you trust as well

愛

(LOVE)

JACKIE PULLINGER SAID...
(SHE IS A MISSIONARY WHO WORKS WITH DRUG ADDICTS IN HONG KONG)

" God wants us to have soft hearts and hard feet. The trouble with so many of us is we have hard hearts and soft feet. "

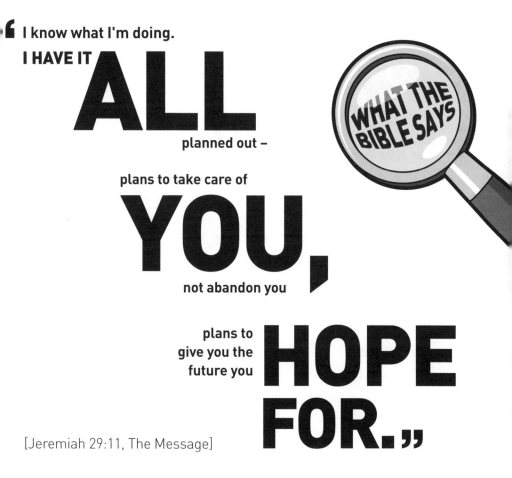

❝ I know what I'm doing.

I HAVE IT ALL

planned out –

plans to take care of

YOU,

not abandon you

plans to
give you the
future you HOPE

FOR.❞

[Jeremiah 29:11, The Message]

WHAT THE BIBLE SAYS

HOW DO YOU FEEL ABOUT THE IDEA OF BEING GUIDED BY GOD?

A SPACE TO **THINK**

WHY DON'T YOU SPEND A FEW MINUTES THINKING ABOUT
THAT AND WRITE DOWN YOUR THOUGHTS ...

WHAT ARE SOME OF THE THINGS YOU WOULD LIKE GOD TO HELP GUIDE
YOU WITH?

Man 9000

In the early 1950s, Chad Varah was the vicar of a very busy church near Clapham Junction in London. He had this idea of a telephone hotline, but he didn't think he was the right person to get it started because he was so busy. So he said to God, 'I'm not the person to do this. I think you need someone from a church in the City' (London's financial district). Churches in the City have very few parishioners, and therefore the vicars have more time available.

A few days later, he was invited to become the vicar of a church exactly like that: the Church of St Stephen's, Walbrook, in the City of London. When he met the patrons of the church and they asked him what he'd do once he was appointed, he said, 'Well, I'd set up a telephone hotline.' They thought it was a great idea.

LOOK!

Chad Varah set up the Samaritans hotline (a phone number that anyone can ring at any time if they are in distress)

On his way to the church, Reverend Varah was thinking: 'What would be the best number for this hotline?' He wanted something that could be easily memorised. He knew that the first three characters would be letters (that was how phone numbers worked back then), so, as the local area was called Mansion House, the letters would be M-A-N. He wondered, 'What could the numbers be, in order to give it a hint of emergency? Something like 999.' He decided that the perfect number would be 'MAN 9000' – easily memorable, with a hint of emergency.

A STORY TO THINK ABOUT

He found the church telephone buried under some rubble in the vestry. Once he salvaged it, he dialled the operator and tried to persuade her to give him the phone number 'MAN 9000'. (It was likely that this number already belonged to someone else.)

When he asked if it might be possible to change the church's number to 'MAN 9000', she explained that it was very unlikely: 'Someone with a number as memorable as that wouldn't change it for love nor money.' Reverend Varah said, 'I have no money, but I have plenty of love! Would you tell me who the number "MAN 9000" belongs to so I can contact them myself?'

The operator asked him where he was calling from, and he realised he didn't even know the church's number. He wiped the dust from the phone handset and saw, in clear print, 'MAN 9000'!

After explaining this coincidence to the operator, Reverend Varah said to God, 'I get the message! You had this planned even before the telephone was installed. Now please stop with the coincidences, because it's getting weird!'

LOOK! ⊗

Somebody calls the Samaritans every 20 seconds

WHAT ABOUT THE HOLY SPIRIT?

WEEKEND
SESSION

THE HOLY SPIRIT HAS OFTEN BEEN MISUNDERSTOOD. WHO DO YOU THINK THE HOLY SPIRIT IS?

Perhaps one of the reasons for the misunderstanding is because older versions of the Bible call him the 'Holy Ghost', which sounds a little scary!

But the Holy Spirit is not a 'ghost' at all – the Holy Spirit is the third person of the Trinity (God – Father, Son and Holy Spirit)

LOOK!

As we spend time with God we become more like him.

72

The Holy Spirit appears throughout the whole Bible

- The Hebrew word for Holy Spirit is 'ruach', which means 'breath'. In Genesis, the Holy Spirit is described as **God's breath** – breathing life into things, including us!

- After Jesus' resurrection, he promised that his disciples would receive the Holy Spirit. On one particular day, now called **Pentecost**, the disciples were praying together and suddenly the Holy Spirit came and filled them in an amazing way. From there they went out and **literally changed the world**!

The Holy Spirit makes us part of God's family

- When we become a Christian, we are made part of God's family, and a family likeness begins to show in our character – this is called, 'the fruit of the spirit' in the Bible

The Holy Spirit gives us gifts

- The Holy Spirit helps us understand God. The Holy Spirit also helps us to pray and gives us 'spiritual gifts'

LOOK! ⊗

The Bible talks about spiritual gifts in 1 Corinthians 12. Each of us is given different gifts to help us play our part in life.

An electric plug on its own is fairly useless – it needs to be connected to a power source. God's Spirit is the power source that we, as Christians, can connect to, and not just as a one-off, but all the time.

FATHER RANIERO CANTALAMESSA SAID...

(CATHOLIC PRIEST AND PREACHER TO THE POPE)

"There is no deep renewal in our lives unless we open ourselves and let the Spirit come into our lives. He wants to. He wants for us to open the door. I hope this day many of you will open the door to the Holy Spirit."

The fruit of the Spirit is
LOVE JOY, PEACE, PATIENCE, KINDNESS, GOODNESS, FAITHFULNESS, GENTLENESS, AND SELF-CONTROL.
Against such things there is no law.

[Galatians 5:22–23]

WHAT THE BIBLE SAYS

DOES THE IDEA OF THE HOLY SPIRIT SEEM POSITIVE TO YOU?

Maybe there are things going on in your life – worries, fears, situations where you'd love someone to come alongside you and help, or just be there with you. The Holy Spirit is the one who draws alongside us, to be the encourager, the comforter and the counsellor.

A SPACE TO THINK

TRY WRITING DOWN SOME THINGS THAT ARE WORRYING YOU AND PUT TODAY'S DATE BY THEM. THEN ASK THE HOLY SPIRIT TO HELP YOU WITH THEM. IN A FEW DAYS OR WEEKS SEE IF THERE HAS BEEN A DIFFERENCE AND WRITE DOWN THE CHANGE AND DATE IT. KEEP ASKING THE HOLY SPIRIT FOR HELP, AND KEEP CHECKING TO SEE WHAT'S HAPPENED AND MAKE A NOTE.

HOW CAN I BE FILLED WITH THE HOLY SPIRIT?

WEEKEND
SESSION

2

WHAT DOES IT MEAN TO BE FILLED WITH THE HOLY SPIRIT?

Is it the same as becoming a Christian?

In the New Testament, Paul writes, 'Be filled with the [Holy] Spirit' (Ephesians 5:18). The original Greek translation of this means, 'go on being filled'.

LOOK! ⊗

God doesn't want us to just have a little bit of his Spirit; he wants us to be filled so that we shine brightly, giving off love and light to those around us.

What happens when people experience the Holy Spirit?

- In the Bible, we see that **good things happen** when people are filled with the Holy Spirit (Acts 10:44–46)

- It's **not all just about feelings** or experiences though. Being filled with the Holy Spirit is about entering into a deeper relationship with Jesus himself

Can anything stop us from being filled?

- God wants to fill all his children with his Holy Spirit, but sometimes we put up barriers that make it difficult for this to happen. We might **feel doubtful, be scared**, or think we're not good enough

But God knew we might think these things, so he told us in the Bible:

- 'Everyone who asks shall receive' – and that means you and me (Luke 11:9–10)

- He is our Father and wants to give us **good gifts** (Luke 11:11–13)

- Jesus said, 'How much more will your Father in heaven give the Holy Spirit to those who ask him!' (Luke 11:13)

- So all we have to do is ask him – **easy!**

> **LOOK!** ⊗
>
> Being filled with the Spirit shouldn't just be a one-off experience: Paul wanted everyone to be constantly filled and refilled.

81

INSTEAD BE FILLED WITH THE SPIRIT.

[Ephesians 5:18]

WHAT THE BIBLE SAYS

IS IT POSSIBLE TO ACTUALLY *LOVE* GOD?

A SPACE TO THINK

WHY DON'T YOU SPEND A FEW MINUTES THINKING ABOUT THAT AND WRITE DOWN YOUR THOUGHTS ...

Shane's story

A STORY TO THINK ABOUT

From the age of fourteen or fifteen, Shane Taylor carried a knife. He had a fascination with guns and knives – mainly knives. He finally got caught, and the charge was Section 20 – GBH. Shane was nineteen. He got Section 20 for two stabbings, a couple of affrays and carrying offensive weapons. He was sentenced to four years.

In his own words Shane describes himself as 'crazy, doing loads of violent and mad things. I was the madman that everyone looked up to – and I had a gang of people who would do what I asked them to do.'

Shane ended up in a maximum-security prison in the segregation unit and finally in the 'CSC' (Close Supervision Centre).

FACT:
The prisoners in the CSC unit are so dangerous that there can be no physical contact between them and the prison officers.

Whilst in prison, he found himself at Alpha. Here's what he had to say about it:

'My intention wasn't to find God. I was thinking, "Free coffee, chocolate biscuits and cake!"

I settled down quite quickly and began to turn up to each of the sessions. I was mostly interested in getting the chocolate biscuits and having little debates, saying things like, "Science proves that it's wrong ..."

Eventually we got to the Holy Spirit day. After we'd watched the talk and had our discussion everyone sat down and we each got prayed for.

The minister, Eddie Baker, put his hand on my head and prayed for me but nothing particularly happened.

Later on I was making a cup of coffee when he came up to me and said, "I've never done this in all the years I've worked here, but I think God is telling me to tell you to come back here this afternoon."

I said, "All right then, I'll come." I remember saying to myself, "If it's real then prove it." I went to the church that afternoon and Eddie was there waiting for me. He picked up a Bible and opened up a few verses where it said something like, "Jesus Christ died on a cross for you. He died for your sins and you can be forgiven."

Then Eddie put his hand on my head and prayed for me. Then he said, "Now you pray."

I said, "What about?"

And he said, "From your heart – let it out and pray."

I said, "Jesus Christ, I know you died on a cross for me. Please, I don't like who I am, please forgive me, please." I said a few other things, which I can't remember now. And then I sat back and we started talking.

As I talked I started to feel a weird feeling in my belly. I thought, "What's that?" But I kept talking to him. Then I started to feel this bubbly feeling slowly coming up my body – through my legs, my chest. When it got to about halfway I started to feel tears coming into my eyes.

I tried to hold it back. I stopped talking, thinking that was going to stop it, because I didn't want to cry. Here I was, a hard man in prison – I didn't want to cry.

But it rose up and up and up until suddenly I began crying my eyes out. I hadn't cried in years. I cried for about five minutes and I could feel a weight being lifted off me because I felt light. Eddie said in a nice voice, "That's the Holy Spirit. It's Jesus."'

Shane attends a local church with his wife Sam. They have two daughters, Angel and Grace. Shane says, 'I never believed God would give me a lovely family. God is great.'

HOW CAN I MAKE THE MOST OF THE REST OF MY LIFE?

WEEKEND SESSION 3

DO YOU KNOW SOMEONE WHO IS LEADING THEIR LIFE WELL? WHAT MAKES THEM STAND OUT TO YOU?

The 'rest of our lives' seems like a pretty long time – but we only get one life, no matter who we are. So it's definitely worth thinking about how we're going to live it – not just what job we'll aim for, but the kind of person that we will be.

What should we do?

- The strange, but amazing thing about God's way of doing things is that it can sometimes seem upside-down in comparison to the ways of the world

- It is tough living for God in today's world, **especially at school**

- The way to make the most of our lives is to **ask God for help**

LOOK! ⊗

It can be easy to let peer pressure squeeze and force us to 'fit the mould' of everyone else. For example, if someone's mean to us, then the standard is that we should be mean back – simple right? But Jesus says we should be loving back ...

How do we live differently?

- We can **pray** to God and offer all areas of our life to him: our time, our dreams, our questions, what we watch, what we look at online, what we say, what we do ... If we do this, we will **live life to the fullest**

- This is not the easiest way to live, but Jesus promises to be with us and give us life (John 10:10)

GOLD

LOOK! ⊗

The secret is to let God improve us from the inside out.

WINNIE THE POOH SAID...
(A.A. MILNE, WROTE WINNIE THE POOH)

" If you live to be a hundred, I want to live to be a hundred minus one day, so I never have to live without you. "

MARK TWAIN SAID...
(MARK TWAIN IS AN AMERICAN AUTHOR WHO WROTE THE ADVENTURES OF TOM SAWYER)

" Sing like no one's listening, love like you've never been hurt, dance like nobody's watching, and live like it's heaven on earth. "

We have all these great people around us as examples. Their lives tell us

WHAT FAITH MEANS.

So we, too, should

RUN THE
RACE that is before us and never quit.

We should remove from our lives anything that would slow us down and the sin that so often makes us fall.

WHAT THE BIBLE SAYS

[Hebrews 12:1, ERV]

HOW DO YOU DEAL WITH PEER PRESSURE?

We can pray to God and offer all areas of our life to him:
our time, our dreams, our questions, what we watch,
what we look at online, what we say, what we do …
If we do this, we will live life to the fullest.

A SPACE TO THINK

WHY DON'T YOU WRITE DOWN YOUR THOUGHTS …

HOW CAN I RESIST EVIL?

SESSION

WHERE DOES EVIL COME FROM?

The New Testament tells us that just as God is behind all that is good in the world, the devil is behind all that is evil.

Why should we believe in the devil?

- It is clear from the horror and evil in our world that the devil exists

- The Bible speaks of him in the Old Testament and in the New Testament

- Beware of taking **too much of an interest** in the devil – that is just as dangerous as doubting that he exists

- The devil's aim is to steal our freedom and destroy us (John 10:10). He wants to prevent us from having a proper relationship with God, and will do anything he can to stop this

LOOK! ⊗

Have you ever noticed that if you add one letter to the word 'God', you get 'good' and if you add one letter to the word 'evil' you get 'devil'?

Should we be worried?

- **No, not at all!** Jesus is all powerful and he has set us free. We have all the forces of heaven on our side, so we have **nothing to fear**

- The Bible tells us that there is a kind of spiritual war going on that we can't see (Ephesians 6.11–12), but when Jesus died on the cross he **won the war**

So how do we attack?

- **By praying.** The Bible says, 'The weapons I fight with are not the weapons the world uses. In fact, it is just the opposite. My weapons have the power of God to destroy the camps of the enemy' (2 Corinthians 10:4, NIrV)

- **By action.** We attack the devil by doing the things that Jesus told us to do (Luke 7:22) and putting on the 'spiritual armour' that God provides us with (Ephesians 6:10–17)

- **By talking.** The devil doesn't want us to be free. He hates it when we pray to God and **tell those we trust** about our struggles, as he knows that this can set us free from guilt, shame and confusion

LOOK!

Jesus has completely defeated the devil, but there are still battles going on, and, as soldiers in God's army we are involved in these (Luke 10:17–20).

C.S. LEWIS SAID...

" There are two equal and opposite errors into which we can fall about the devils. One is to disbelieve in their existence; the other is to believe and to feel an excessive and unhealthy interest in them. They themselves are equally pleased by both errors. "

Don't let evil overcome you.

OVERCOME

evil by doing good.

[Romans 12:21, NIrV]

WHY DO YOU THINK THE WORLD IS IN SUCH A MESS?

The story of Corrie ten Boom

A STORY TO THINK ABOUT

Corrie ten Boom was a Dutch Christian, who survived the Holocaust in World War II. She had been imprisoned in the Nazi concentration camps during World War II because she and her family had been hiding Jews and helping them escape from the Nazis. One of the concentration camps that she and her sister, Betsie, were imprisoned in was called Ravensbrück. Betsie died in this concentration camp.

After the war, Corrie travelled the world, speaking about her experience. Here is what happened to her on one such occasion:

'It was at a church service in Munich that I saw him, a former S.S. man who had stood guard at the shower room door in the processing center at Ravensbrück. He was the first of our actual jailers that I had seen since that time. And suddenly it was all there – the roomful of mocking men, the heaps of clothing, Betsie's pain-blanched face.

He came up to me as the church was emptying, beaming and bowing. "How grateful I am for your message, Fraulein." He said. "To think that, as you say, He has washed my sins away!" His hand was thrust out to shake mine. And I, who had preached so often to the people in Bloemendaal the need to forgive, kept my hand at my side.

Even as the angry, vengeful thoughts boiled through me, I saw the sin of them. Jesus Christ had died for this man; was I going to ask for more? "Lord Jesus", I prayed, "forgive me and help me to forgive him." I tried to smile, I struggled to raise my hand. I could not. I felt nothing, not the slightest spark of warmth or charity. And so again I breathed a silent prayer. "Jesus", I prayed, "I cannot forgive him. Give me your forgiveness."

As I took his hand the most incredible thing happened. From my shoulder along my arm and through my hand a current seemed to pass from me to him, while into my heart sprang a love for this stranger that almost overwhelmed me. And so I discovered that it is not on our forgiveness any more than on our goodness that the world's healing hinges, but on His. When He tells us to love our enemies, He gives – along with the command, the love itself.'

Adapted from www.ecclesia.org/truth/corrie

WHY AND HOW SHOULD I TELL OTHERS?

SESSION

THINK ABOUT ONE OF THE BEST THINGS THAT HAS EVER HAPPENED TO YOU – HOW QUICKLY DID YOU WANT TO SHARE YOUR GOOD NEWS WITH SOMEONE ELSE?

Why should we tell other people about our faith in Jesus?

- **ONE REASON**

  Because **Jesus wants us to**. After he rose from the dead, he said to go and tell everyone the amazing news that they can be forgiven; they can be **set free** from the bad stuff holding them back; they can have eternal life.

- **ANOTHER REASON**

  Because we love our friends and family. **Love** must be what motivates us, because we want people to discover all the joy, peace and new life that we have found in Jesus.

- **A THIRD REASON**

  Because it is good news! We **can't just keep it** to ourselves.

Right from the start, it is good to recognise **two possible extremes**: either trying to force our views down other people's throats or keeping silent and never telling anyone about our faith.

The key to avoiding these two extremes is to **really care** about the person you are telling, and to trust God.

Ask God about what you should say or do and the Holy Spirit will show you when the time is right. He may just want you to **be a good friend**, or simply invite them to your youth group or church.

HOW CAN WE SHARE OUR FAITH?

Live the message

- How we behave and what we say and do, should line up with how we believe Jesus wants us to be. We are **called by God** to love those around us, to love the poor and to stand up against injustice

LOOK!

If you don't know the answer to a question someone asks you about God, **don't worry**, and don't pretend you do! Just be willing to go away and find out. Some questions are so huge, that even though there are lots of books written on them, still no one has an absolute answer for them!

Talk the message

- There is no formula for how to speak about your faith – the important thing is to tell your story and **just be natural**. Never use force and don't pressurise people, or they might not want to talk to you about it again

Present the message

- It is easy to think, 'What difference could I possibly make?' But we are all simply called to tell people about our **personal** experience of God – people love hearing others' stories

Trust the message

- God still does **miracles** today, and we shouldn't be afraid to ask him to show his power to people through miracles – big and small!

Pray the message

- We can pray that people would be open to the truth about God and that God would give us **courage** to start talking about our faith, or that someone would just ask us first!

SINÉAD O'CONNOR SAID...
(SHE IS AN IRISH SINGER-SONGWRITER
WHO SANG 'NOTHING COMPARES 2 U')

" As a race we feel empty because our spirituality has been wiped out and we don't know how to express ourselves. And as a result we're encouraged to fill that gap with alcohol, drugs, sex or money. People out there are screaming for the truth. "

SAINT FRANCIS
OF ASSISI SAID...
(1182-1226)

" Preach the gospel at all times; if necessary, use words. "

But before people can pray to the Lord for help, they **MUST BELIEVE IN HIM.** And before they can believe in the Lord, they must **HEAR ABOUT HIM.** And for anyone to hear about the Lord,

SOMEONE MUST TELL THEM.

And before anyone can go and tell them, they must

BE SENT.

As the Scriptures say, "How wonderful it is to see someone coming to tell good news!"

[Romans 10:14–15, ERV]

WHAT THE BIBLE SAYS

IF YOU DID NOT KNOW ANYTHING AT ALL ABOUT CHRISTIANITY, HOW WOULD YOU LIKE TO FIND OUT ABOUT IT?

One starfish at a time

A STORY TO THINK ABOUT

A man was walking along a beach in Mexico when he saw a remarkable sight – the beach was covered in tens of thousands of starfish! The tide had gone out and left them stranded on the beach, dying in the heat of the sun. The man saw a young boy standing among the starfish. The boy was picking them up one at a time, running down to the sea and throwing them into the water, before going back to get another starfish and repeating the process again.

The man went up to him and said, 'Look, can't you see – there are tens of thousands of starfish out here! I don't really think what you're doing is going to make any difference.'

The young boy picked up another starfish, went down to the water's edge, threw it in the sea and said, 'I bet it made a difference for that one!'

We may not be able to change the world on our own, but we can help the lives of people around us, one by one.

A SPACE TO THINK

COULD YOU TRY DOING ONE OF THESE IN THE NEXT WEEK?

- PRAY FOR A FRIEND
- MAKE AN EFFORT TO TALK TO A LONELY OR BULLIED PERSON AT SCHOOL
- ASK A FRIEND TO A YOUTH EVENT AT YOUR CHURCH
- ASK GOD TO GIVE YOU THE OPPORTUNITY TO TELL SOMEBODY THE STORY OF HOW YOU CAME TO BE A CHRISTIAN

113

DOES GOD HEAL TODAY?

SESSION

9

DO YOU BELIEVE THAT GOD CAN HEAL PEOPLE TODAY?

Healing in the Bible

- If we read the Bible we will see that **God heals** people. A quarter of the Gospels are about healing!

- God said in the Old Testament, 'I am the God who heals you' (Exodus 15:26)

- Jesus sent his disciples out to **pray for healing**. As Jesus went up to heaven, he told his disciples to go and do what he did (Matthew 28:16–20)

- So that includes all Christians today

Healing in History

- The earliest churches believed healing was possible and so, like the original disciples, they just went ahead and prayed for it. The church has been praying for the sick and seeing **God perform miracles** ever since

How do we pray for healing?

- Our job is to pray and **ask God to heal** – it is God who then does the healing

- Prayers for healing should be simple, not long and complicated. Remember, it is God's power, not the number of our words, that heal

- If nothing seems to happen or if the person is only partially healed, **don't give up**. Even Jesus sometimes had to pray twice (Mark 8:22–26)! We shouldn't feel discouraged if we need to keep praying

- When healing doesn't happen, we need to remember that we still have to wait to see the kingdom of God come fully on earth, which will be when Jesus returns. What does that mean exactly? **It's tricky**, but essentially it means that when Jesus came to earth around 2000 years ago, the healings he did were a sign that the kingdom of God had arrived, but it hasn't yet fully arrived

> **LOOK!** ⊗
>
> God can heal our bodies, and he can also heal other types of hurts too, whether it's emotional pain or any other kind of pain. Nothing is impossible for God.

PATRICK PEARSON MILES...
(HAS 'CHRONIC RENAL FAILURE' WHICH BASICALLY MEANS HIS KIDNEYS DON'T WORK AT ALL - HE HASN'T HAD A PEE SINCE 1994! HE DEVELOPED KIDNEY DISEASE AGED 17; 10 YEARS LATER HIS KIDNEYS PACKED UP). HE SAID THIS:

> God does not give, or even allow, sickness in order to teach us something. However, he turns all things for good for those who love him. So if you are sick, ask God what he wants to teach you through it and how you can bless others as a result. The devil is the author of sickness and his plan is to make you blame God and turn from him and make you focus on yourself and your sickness and how unfair it all is. Pray and seek your healing from the living God who heals. It's part of his DNA to heal, so praying these prayers are in line with his character – but be patient, and persistent, pursuing him, as his timing is very often different to ours. Seek first *his* kingdom.

" I am the

THE
LORD who
HEALS YOU. "

[Exodus 15:26]

119

WHY DO YOU THINK JESUS HEALED PEOPLE?

WHY DON'T YOU SPEND A FEW MINUTES THINKING ABOUT THAT AND WRITE DOWN YOUR THOUGHTS ...

A SPACE TO THINK

Ajay's Story

Ajay Gohill was born in Kenya but moved to England in 1971. He was brought up as a Hindu and worked in the family business as a newsagent in Neasden. At the age of twenty-one he contracted Erythrodermic Psoriasis, a chronic skin disease. His weight dropped from 11.5 stone [73 kg] to 7.5 stone [47.5 kg]. He received treatment all over the world – in the United States, Germany, Switzerland and Israel, as well as all over England. He spent 80 per cent of his earnings trying to find a cure and took strong drugs which affected his liver. Eventually, he had to give up his job. The disease covered his body from head to toe; he says he was so horrible to look at, he couldn't even wear a t-shirt. He lost all his friends, and his wife and son left him. He wanted to die.

One October, Ajay was lying in his hospital bed. He cried out, 'God, if you are watching, let me die – I am sorry if I have done something wrong.' From his locker he pulled out a Good News Bible. He opened it at random and read Psalm 38:

'O Lord, don't punish me in your anger! You have wounded me with your arrows; you have struck me down. Because of your anger, I am in great pain; my whole body is diseased because of my sins. I am drowning in the flood of my sins; they are a burden too heavy to bear. Because I have been foolish, my sores stink and rot. I am bowed down, I am crushed; I mourn all day long.

I am burning with fever and I am near to death. I am worn out and utterly crushed; my heart is troubled and I groan with pain. O Lord, you know what I long for; you hear all my groans. My heart is pounding, my strength is gone, and my eyes have lost their brightness. My friends and neighbours will not come near me, because of my sores; even my family keeps away from me ... Do not abandon me, O God; do not stay away from me, my God! Help me now, O Lord my saviour!' (Psalm 38:1–11, 21–22, Good News Bible).

Each and every verse seemed relevant to him. He prayed for God to heal him, and then he fell into a deep sleep. When he awoke the next morning 'everything looked new'. He took a bath and when he looked at the water, he saw his skin had lifted off his body and was floating. He called in the nurses and told them that God was healing him: all of his skin was new, like a baby's. He was totally healed and has since been reunited with his son. Ajay says that the inner healing that has taken place in his life is even greater than the physical healing. He says, 'Every day I live for Jesus. I am his servant today.'

A STORY TO THINK ABOUT

Ali's Story

'From the age of about 15–19, I had around 33 warts on my right hand. Some were quite painful. They were really quite visible and obvious on my hand and I was super-aware of them. I tried everything to get them to go, from creams to having them painfully iced at the doctors, but they never seemed to budge. I remember my mum saying she'd like to pray for them but I remember also getting quite annoyed with her and saying, What difference would that make? Didn't she realise how painful and deep rooted they were? I didn't really believe in the reality of God then and am certainly sure I didn't believe in the power of prayer. The people at my work during my gap year even teased me and called me leper, refusing to shake my hand sometimes, all in jest but it definitely got to me after a while ...

That summer, at the end of my gap year, I went on a trip with the youth group I was loosely involved with, to Tanzania, which was really eye-opening and great fun. Because of work commitments I had to come back a week earlier than all the other youth. Half way through that week, I woke up one day and over the course of the day was able to just peel my warts off my hand with no pain. It was almost as if there was some special liquid on them and by the end of the day they'd all come off.

What was awesome was that the next day it was almost as if they'd not been there at all, no scars ...

I thought it was cool and when the youth group came back, including my 16 year old sister, I mentioned to her that, 'by the way my warts have all gone.'

She said to me that she'd really felt that she should pray for my warts while out in Africa, and had got the whole youth group together to pray, and lo and behold at the same time, the same week, they'd all come off my hand.

I dismissed it as coincidence but I remember her challenging me and saying no, this time I couldn't just dismiss it, that she felt it was God showing how real and powerful he was to me ... and for the first time in my life, I think I truly believed in a God who was real, powerful and able to change things in my life, and a God who heard our prayers and had the power to heal.'

A STORY TO THINK ABOUT

WHAT ABOUT THE CHURCH?

SESSION

WHAT IS THE CHURCH? JUST ANOTHER CLUB? A TYPE OF BUILDING? SOMEWHERE TO WASTE A COUPLE OF HOURS ON A SUNDAY MORNING? POINTLESS...?

OR, IS IT MUCH, MUCH MORE...?

Jesus was passionate about the church and the New Testament is packed full of images of what the church should be like. Here are a few:

The people of God

- The Bible tells us that the 'church' is **made up of people**, not buildings (1 Peter 2:9)

- It's a great idea to join a church and to be part of a Christian youth group. It's about having **friendships** with other people to encourage and help each other

LOOK!

Being a Christian is about having a relationship with God, but it is also about having relationships with other people.

The family of God

- Have you heard the saying, 'You can choose your friends but you can't choose your family'? It's the same with the family of God – we may be very different and we might find it hard to get along with some people, but we are called to **love one another** and **forgive one another**

- Sometimes family members **argue**. It's the same in the church. Denominations do not always agree, but we are all still part of God's family and should try and focus on the things we agree do about

The body of Christ

- Just as different parts of the human body have their own jobs to do, we are all given **different gifts** by God to use in the church

- We can ask God to show us our gifts so we can play our part in God's family. We might have the gift of **encouraging others** or a passion for justice and fairness

LOOK! ⊗

Do you ever get really upset deep inside when you see someone being bullied at school? That's because it's not fair and God has given you compassion for them.

ABRAHAM LINCOLN SAID...
(ABRAHAM LINCOLN WAS PRESIDENT OF
THE USA, 1861–1865)

" If all the people who fell asleep in church on Sunday morning were laid out end to end ... they would be a great deal more comfortable. "

But you are a

CHOSEN
PEOPLE, a ROYAL priesthood,
A HOLY
NATION,
a people belonging to God.

WHAT THE BIBLE SAYS

[1 Peter 2:9]

WHAT PART ARE YOU GOING TO PLAY IN GOD'S CHURCH?

What do you think your gifts from God are?

A SPACE TO THINK

WHY DON'T YOU SPEND A FEW MINUTES THINKING ABOUT THAT AND THEN PUT A CIRCLE AROUND THE ONES YOU THINK YOU HAVE ... OR WOULD LIKE! THEN ASK GOD FOR THAT GIFT.

CARING · GIVING
ENCOURAGING
JOY WISDOM
PROPHECY
KNOWLEDGE
MERCY · SERVING
GIVING · PRAYING
DISCERNMENT
FRIENDSHIP HELP
HOSPITALITY
LEADERSHIP
TEACHING FAITH
HEALING · · · · · ·

PRAYER OF COMMITMENT

The judge and his friend

There were once two little boys who were best friends. They played together, went to school together, they even went to university together. They were inseparable, until their careers took them in very different directions.

One became a lawyer, the other a criminal. While one eventually became a judge, the other disappeared deeper and deeper into a life of crime. Eventually the criminal was caught and sent to trial.

On the fateful day in the courtroom, he came face to face with his old, best friend the judge.

So the judge had a dilemma. He loved his friend but he had to do justice.

So the judge handed down the appropriate penalty for the offence – a huge fine. There was no way that his old friend could ever afford to pay what he owed.

But then the judge took off his robes, went down, stood with his friend, and wrote out a cheque covering the cost.

He paid the penalty himself.

That, in a way, is a bit like us and God. God loves us, but at the same time, there needed to be a price paid for the bad stuff we have done. God can't just say (just like that judge couldn't just say), 'It's okay, don't worry about it,' because it's not okay. But like the judge, God paid the penalty himself – through Jesus.

Jesus' death on the cross took away our bad stuff and made us clean again.

It means that God is no longer separated from us, and we can begin a relationship with him

It says in the Bible 'God loved the world so much that he gave his one and only Son. Anyone who believes in him will not die but will have eternal life.' John 3:16 (NIrV)

If you feel that you would like to ask Jesus to come into your life and to forgive your sins, then here is a short prayer that you can say.

> *Father in Heaven, I don't know you or your love, but I want to. Lord Jesus, I want to follow you from today and for you to be my friend. Thank you for the true life and forgiveness you won for me on the cross: the freedom and the life I was born for. Holy Spirit please bring God's love to my heart now. I am yours forever.*
>
> *Amen.*

If you said that prayer, then tell someone who is a Christian about it – maybe someone in your church, or your youth group leader or a family member.

HANDY L👓K UP PAGE

There might be some phrases or words that we've put in the chapters that make you think 'what on earth are they talking about?' – so we've tried to define some of them here to help you out.

Where you see a word in the book coloured in like this then *you'll be able to look it up below:*

AMEN

Christians finish their prayers by saying 'in the name of Jesus. Amen.' Amen is a Hebrew word. It means 'so be it' (or 'God, please answer my prayer!'). We pray 'in the name of Jesus' – because he is the reason that we can talk openly to God.

ARCHBISHOP

This is the title given to the chief bishop – he oversees all the other Church of England clerics.

THE BIBLE

This is the book that Christians refer to and believe is God's word – you can learn more about it in Session 5. It is one big book that is made up of sixty-six little books (quite often named after the person who wrote the book, but sometimes named after the place, or people that it was written to.)

The Bible is split into two sections – the Old Testament and the New Testament.

BIBLE REFERENCES (EG, JOHN 14:6)

Where we've put something like 'John 14:6' we're referring to a passage in the Bible – the word or name is the name of the book in the Bible (there are lots), then the first number is the chapter in that book, and the second number is the verse in the chapter. Get a Bible and have a look, then you'll see what we mean.

CHRISTIANITY

The belief in the gospel of Jesus Christ.

CHRISTIANS

These people are followers of Jesus Christ (Christ-ians).

CHURCH

Church can refer to a building where services are held, but 'the church' is actually the name for all Christians together; It's the family of God.

THE CROSS

Jesus was put to death on a cross. The cross was basically two huge planks of wood in the shape of a cross. Jesus' hands were nailed to the horizontal plank and his feet were nailed to the vertical one. He was left hanging there until he died. This form of execution was called crucifixion.

CRUCIFIXION

See under 'the cross'.

DENOMINATIONS

These are different groups within Christianity eg, Baptist, Roman Catholic, Church of England, Pentecostal, Orthodox. Different denominations often have a distinct style of doing church, such as style of worship, communion and prayers.

THE DEVIL

Sometimes referred to as Satan. The devil is described as a liar and the father of lies. He is described in the Bible as a fallen angel. His ultimate goal is to lead people away from God.

FAITH

Choosing to trust and believe in something that you can't immediately see or touch. Faith is like trust.

THE GOSPEL

This is the good news of Jesus Christ, who came to earth to reveal God the father to us and to save us from our sins. God sent him to take on the punishment for our sins, to die instead of us, so that we can call God Father and receive the gift of eternal life in heaven. That's the gospel, and it's all because of Jesus.

GOSPELS

These are the first four books of the New Testament: Matthew, Mark, Luke and John. They are called the Gospels because they all tell the story of the good news of Jesus Christ (his birth, his life, his death and resurrection). Gospel translates from the Greek word *'euangelion'*, which means 'good news'.

HOLOCAUST (WORLD WAR II)

The mass killing of approximately six million European Jews during World War II, a programme of systematic, state-sponsored murder by Nazi Germany, led by Adolf Hitler, throughout Nazi-occupied territory. Of the nine million Jews who had resided in Europe before the Holocaust, approximately two-thirds were killed. (http://en.wikipedia.org/wiki/The_Holocaust)

HOLY SPIRIT

The third person of the Trinity, the Spirit of God. When we become Christians, the Holy Spirit comes to live inside of us. The Holy Spirit helps us to feel God's presence in our lives and also helps us to hear God's voice and think of the words to say to God. (Plus a whole lot more. See Weekend sessions 1 and 2).

JESUS CHRIST

Jesus was the Son of God – you can learn more about him in sessions 1 and 2.

MATTHEW, MARK, LUKE, JOHN

See under 'Gospels'.

THE NEW TESTAMENT

A record of everything that happened from Jesus Christ's birth to a little time after his death. It includes the teaching and miracles of Jesus and talks about how we should live our lives, even now.

THE OLD TESTAMENT

This is the first part of the Bible. It is ... well ... really old and it records stuff that happened before Jesus Christ was born.

THE POPE

The Pope is head of the Roman Catholic Church and is the Bishop of Rome. He lives in the Vatican in the Vatican City which is in Rome, Italy.

PROPHECY/PROPHECIES

A prediction or foretelling of the future. In Christianity it is often a message of truth that reveals God's will for a person or a group of people. Christian prophecy should be uplifting and encouraging and is one of the spiritual gifts.

RESURRECTION

After Jesus was crucified on the cross, he was buried in a grave. But after being dead for three days – he came back to life. He appeared to quite a few people but after that he went to be with God in heaven. This is called the resurrection.

REVEREND

The official title given to vicars in the Church of England. In some churches they are also called pastors.

SIN

The bad stuff that we all do. Maybe it's being mean to someone, or being jealous of someone – so not just the serious stuff that we can go to prison for.

TRINITY

This is the word used to describe God the Father, Jesus the Son, and the Holy Spirit. It is something that is three (Father, Son, Holy Spirit) but also one (God) – a bit like water, ice and steam – all are H_2O, but each is different too.